Farm Animals
Sheep

By Rebecca Sabelko

BELLWETHER MEDIA • MINNEAPOLIS, MN

BLASTOFF! Beginners

Blastoff! Beginners are developed by literacy experts and educators to meet the needs of early readers. These engaging informational texts support young children as they begin reading about their world. Through simple language and high frequency words paired with crisp, colorful photos, Blastoff! Beginners launch young readers into the universe of independent reading.

Sight Words in This Book

are	eat	on	time
be	from	run	to
big	have	some	too
black	in	the	white
brown	is	these	
can	it	they	

This edition first published in 2024 by Bellwether Media, Inc.

No part of this publication may be reproduced in whole or in part without written permission of the publisher. For information regarding permission, write to Bellwether Media, Inc., Attention: Permissions Department, 6012 Blue Circle Drive, Minnetonka, MN 55343.

Library of Congress Cataloging-in-Publication Data

Names: Sabelko, Rebecca, author.
Title: Sheep / by Rebecca Sabelko.
Description: Minneapolis, MN : Bellwether Media, 2024. | Series: Blastoff! Beginners: Farm Animals | Includes bibliographical references and index. | Audience: Ages 4-7 | Audience: Grades K-1
Identifiers: LCCN 2023039754 | ISBN 9798886877649 (library binding) | ISBN 9798886879520 (paperback) | ISBN 9798886878585 (ebook)
Subjects: LCSH: Sheep--Juvenile literature. | Farm life--Juvenile literature.
Classification: LCC SF375.2 .S23 2024 | DDC 636.3--dc23
LC record available at https://lccn.loc.gov/2023039754

Text copyright © 2024 by Bellwether Media, Inc. BLASTOFF! BEGINNERS and associated logos are trademarks and/or registered trademarks of Bellwether Media, Inc.

Editor: Elizabeth Neuenfeldt   Designer: Laura Sowers

Printed in the United States of America, North Mankato, MN.

Table of Contents

Wool in Spring!	4
What Are Sheep?	6
Life on the Farm	14
Sheep Facts	22
Glossary	23
To Learn More	24
Index	24

Wool in Spring!

It is spring. The farmer cuts the sheep's thick **wool**!

wool

What Are Sheep?

Sheep are big farm animals.

They have wool.
It can be white,
brown, gray,
or black.

Some sheep have **horns**. Horns can be big!

Sheep have **split hooves**. They move easily on rocky ground.

Life on the Farm

Sheep stay in **flocks**.
They eat grass.
They eat hay.

flock

grass

hay

Farmers cut wool from sheep. Wool becomes clothes!

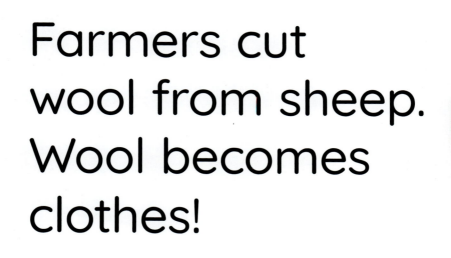

Sheep give milk, too. The milk often becomes cheese!

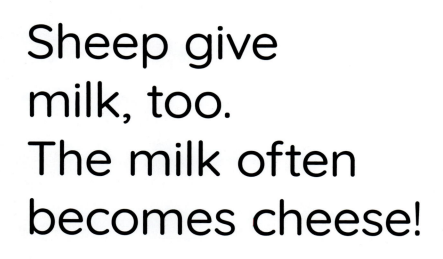

cheese

These sheep run to the barn. Time to eat. Baa, baa!

barn

Sheep Facts

Parts of a Sheep

thick wool

horns

split hooves

Life on the Farm

eat

give wool

give milk

Glossary

flocks

groups of sheep

horns

hard parts on the heads of some sheep

split hooves

hard foot coverings that have two parts

wool

the soft, thick hair of sheep

To Learn More

ON THE WEB

FACTSURFER

Factsurfer.com gives you a safe, fun way to find more information.

1. Go to www.factsurfer.com.

2. Enter "sheep" into the search box and click 🔍.

3. Select your book cover to see a list of related content.

Index

barn, 20
cheese, 18
clothes, 16
colors, 8
cuts, 4, 16
eat, 14, 20
farm, 6

farmer, 4, 5, 16
flocks, 14, 15
grass, 14, 15
hay, 14, 15
horns, 10, 11
milk, 18
run, 20

size, 6, 10
split hooves, 12, 13
spring, 4
wool, 4, 8, 16

The images in this book are reproduced through the courtesy of: Eric Isselee, cover, pp. 6, 7; photomaster, pp. 3, 22; New Africa, p. 4; :bbbrrn, pp. 4-5; WeStudio, pp. 8-9; Twinsterphoto, pp. 10-11; Edaccor, pp. 12-13; Mimadeo, pp. 14-15; Sheryl Watson, p. 15 (grass); Oleksiichik, p. 15 (hay); esemelwe, p. 16; Photographer and Illustrator, pp. 16-17; fabiano goreme caddeo, p. 18; Cavan Images/ Alamy, pp. 18-19; MaryShutterstock, p. 20; Redzaal, pp. 20-21; Rezza Photos, p. 22 (eat); Terelyuk, p. 22 (give wool); Gutescu Eduard, p. 22 (give milk); brackish_nz, p. 23 (flocks); wk1003mike, p. 23 (horns); Jonathan Oscar, p. 23 (split hooves); SKT Studio, p. 23 (wool).